GAT

Mediterranean Diet for beginners

The 7-DAY meal plan, Easy start for WEIGHT LOSS

Olivia Goodwin

Text Copyright © Olivia Goodwin

All rights reserved. No part of this guide may be reproduced in any form without permission in writing from the publisher except in the case of brief quotations embodied in critical articles or reviews.

Legal & Disclaimer

The information contained in this book and its contents is not designed to replace or take the place of any form of medical or professional advice; and is not meant to replace the need for independent medical, financial, legal or other professional advice or services, as may be required. The content and information in this book has been provided for educational and entertainment purposes only.

The content and information contained in this book has been compiled from sources deemed reliable, and it is accurate to the best of the Author's knowledge, information and belief. However, the Author cannot guarantee its accuracy and validity and cannot be held liable for any errors and/or omissions. Further, changes are periodically made to this book as and when needed. Where appropriate and/or necessary, you must consult a professional (including but not limited to your doctor, attorney, financial advisor or such other professional advisor) before using any of the suggested remedies, techniques, or information in this book.

Upon using the contents and information contained in this book, you agree to hold harmless the Author from and against any damages, costs, and expenses, including any legal fees potentially resulting from the application of any of the information provided by this book. This disclaimer applies to any loss, damages or injury caused by the use and application, whether directly or indirectly, of any advice or information presented, whether for breach of contract, tort, negligence, personal injury, criminal intent, or under any other cause of action.

You agree to accept all risks of using the information presented inside this book.

You agree that by continuing to read this book, where appropriate and/or necessary, you shall consult a professional (including but not limited to your doctor, attorney, or financial advisor or such other advisor as needed) before using any of the suggested remedies, techniques, or information in this book.

Table of Contents

Text Copyright © Olivia Goodwin 1
Table of Contents 2
Introduction 5
What is the Mediterranean Diet? 6
MEDITERRANEAN DIET PYRAMID 8
Health Benefits of the Mediterranean Diet 10
Reasons Why the Mediterranean Diet Truly Works for Weight Loss 12
HOW the MEDITERRANEAN Diet HELP with WEIGHT LOSS 13
The Importance of Exercise 15
7-DAY SAMPLE MEAL PLAN EXAMPLE 17
HEALTHY BREAKFAST 20
Strawberry breakfast 21
Watermelon Gazpacho 22
Strawberry-citrus soup 23
Omelet with vegetables and herbs 24
Omelet with chicken breast 25
Egg baked in avocado 26
Italian frittata with vegetables 27
Pita bread rolls with bean salad and avocado 28
Greek style pumpkin 29
Stuffed sweet potatoes 30
Cauliflower with cream cheese and chicken 31
FRUIT and BERRY DISHES 32
Fresh Berry soufflé 33

Cottage cheese - lime soufflé ... 34
Bananas in batter ... 35
Grilled Fruits ... 36
Strawberry soufflé ... 37
Fresh pear soup ... 38
Cheesecake with berries ... 39
Fruity smoothies ... 40
Berry smoothies ... 41
Smoothies with plum, banana, and orange ... 42
Mango, strawberry and Chia seeds ... 43
Sherbet with melon and apple ... 44
FISH and SEAFOOD ... 45
Ceviche with langoustines ... 46
Baked lobster with herbs ... 47
Trout baked with vegetables ... 48
Provence Dorade with Tapenade ... 49
Delicious shrimp ... 50
Baked seafood with vegetables and lemon ... 51
Mussels with vegetables ... 52
PASTA & SOUPS ... 53
Baked pasta with minced meat ... 54
Lasagne alla Bolognese ... 55
Manicotti with light pasta sauce ... 56
Spaghetti Carbonara ... 57
Pasta with low-fat cheese ... 58
Pasta with salmon and shrimp ... 59

Gazpacho with tomato juice and Tabasco sauce 60
Cream soup with pumpkin and French bean 61
Vegetable cream soup 62
Green cream soup 63
HEALTHY SALADS 64
Salad with avocado, pineapple, and onions 65
Salad with shrimp 66
Salad with watermelon, cheese, and fresh basil 67
Salad with fresh vegetables 68
Salad with cod liver and quail eggs 69
Salad with shrimps and olives 70
Salad with lentils and avocado 71
Salad with Brussels sprouts, apples and nuts 72
Salad with shrimps and quail eggs 73
Salad with lentils and trout 74
Conclusion 75
Author's Afterthoughts 76

Introduction

Our strong health and healthy eating are dependent on each other. From ancient times people paid attention to food. In ancient China, according to historians, the Chinese tried to find the golden formula of eternal youth, paying attention to the ratio of vegetable components of food, and its effect on the health and weight of a person.

Healthy eating is one of the fundamental moments of a healthy lifestyle and, therefore, preserving and strengthening your health. This is an essential and constantly acting factor, ensuring adequate growth and development of the body. A healthy diet provides a harmonious physical and neuropsychological development, increases resistance to infectious diseases and resistance to unfavorable environmental conditions.

Food is one of the most important environmental factors that affect health, working capacity, mental and physical development, as well as the life expectancy of a person. Our body must receive all the important nutrients, vitamins, and minerals. Therefore, it is especially important to eat vegetables, fruits, cereals, and herbs. In addition, from the food, our body receives the necessary for life, proteins, fats, carbohydrates, as well as biologically active substances, vitamins, and mineral salts.

Dietitians are sure that the menu of any person, especially a child, should be diverse. It should include all products that are necessary for a person. It has long been known to everyone that the condition of the skin of the hair, the activity of our organs and systems, largely depends on a healthy diet that contains all the necessary substances in certain quantities.

Therefore, if you are a fan of different dishes and really want to lose weight fast, this means that you will definitely like my book and it will be an indispensable addition to your kitchen. In my book, you will find recipes for simple, useful, tasty, and super-fast dishes for every day. In addition, step-by-step instructions and bright illustrations will help you quickly learn how to prepare truly culinary masterpieces that will make any day special!

Doubtless, the healthy diet can reduce weight, improve health and cleanse the body of toxins. However, do not forget that before starting a diet, you need to check the condition of all organs and body systems. Otherwise, the harm of a diet can be irreparable.

What is the Mediterranean Diet?

Scientists have noticed that people do not suffer from atherosclerosis, cardiovascular diseases and complicating disease, for example, myocardial infarction and strokes in the Mediterranean countries. In addition, people in these countries live 10 to 15 years longer than in other countries of the world. What is the reason for the phenomenon of low mortality from cardiovascular diseases and longevity of the population? The answer to this question is not simple. The causes can also be found in the peculiarities of a favorable climate, in genetical inheritance, and in the social conditions of life, etc.

Specialists and nutritionists see the reason for the absence of cardiovascular diseases and their complicating disease in the Mediterranean region, especially in a special food system. Of course, people in Spain, Portugal, Italy, and Greece do not eat the same way. Nevertheless, there is a reason to talk about the impact of the Mediterranean diet.

The first popularizers of the Mediterranean diet were American doctors Ansel Kies and Walter Willet. Thanks to their efforts, the mistrust of Mediterranean diet was overcome! Of course, at first, nobody could understand how food rich in carbohydrates, generously flavored with olive oil and washed down with red wine, helps not only to lose weight but also to protect health.

It is related to the fact that a significant proportion of vegetables, fruits, berries, and juices from them in the daily diet characterizes this diet. Traditional cuisine for people from Mediterranean countries is the use of a large number of seasonal vegetables and fruits, herbs, legumes, nuts, whole grain cereals and bread, pasta from the grains of durum wheat. Citizens consume many sea fish and seafood.

In the diet must be present olive oil! They very often use in cooking olives and olives, which are part of almost any dish. The nutrition almost does not contain adipose! Olive oil is constantly present during breakfast, lunch, and dinner. It is used for all kinds of salads from vegetables and seafood, and for roasting different foods. At the same time, the Mediterranean diet does not cause heartburn, in contrast to dishes cooked with lard.

Olive oil reduces the level of cholesterol in the blood and delays the development of the atherosclerotic process due to the unsaturated fatty acids and vitamin E. In addition, olive oil promotes regular work of the intestines, which is very important for diseases of the cardiovascular system, which are often accompanied by coprostasia. In addition, olive oil is also useful for dyskinesia of the biliary tract, since it is a choleretic agent.

In addition to it, citizens use mostly natural sour-milk products such as yogurt, skim yogurt, soft cheeses with low-fat content, for example, feta and mozzarella. Milk or milk dishes in the diet is a rarity.

Local residents really like a red wine of good quality and only local production! However, they are not interested in pastries, confectionery, and sweets. As a rule, preference is given to natural products, for example, nuts, dried fruits, and honey.

People in this region lead an active lifestyle! They are optimistic, emotional and little susceptible to various diseases. Their secret is a healthy diet! The Mediterranean diet deserves a positive attitude of nutritionists primarily as a vegetarian diet.

This is why the Mediterranean diet can easily reduce weight, improve health and cleanse the body of toxins. However, before using a diet you must take into account the metabolic, genetic characteristics of your body. Do not forget that before being on a diet, you need to check the condition of all organs and body systems. Otherwise, the harm of a diet can be irreparable. Take care and be healthy!

MEDITERRANEAN DIET PYRAMID

Less Often
Meats and Sweets

Weekly: Moderate Portions
Poultry, Eggs, Cheese and Yogurt

Often: at least Twice each Week
Fish and Seafood

Every Day: Base Each Meal Around these Foods
Vegetables, Fruits, Whole Wheat Grains, Olive Oil, Beans, Nuts, Legumes and Seeds, Herbs and Spices

Mediterranean Diet Pyramid

Doctors of different nationalities and regions have long been trying to find the ideal diet when both nutrition is balanced, and hunger does not excruciate, and weight regularly melts without harm to health.

Dietitians and doctors from the Mediterranean made tremendous strides in this process, which constituted a unique and effective Food Pyramid, helping to lose weight gradually without stress for the body, starvation and depressed mood.

The pyramid is designed in such a way that the usual products necessary in life are not completely excluded but replaced by more useful analogs, for example, fat, margarine is replaced by useful olive and linseed vegetable oil. Today you do not need to count calories and carefully measure the proportions! Now when creating the menu, you can focus on a simple and convenient pyramid of products!

The pyramid is developed based on researches and conclusions of doctors. In addition to healthy foods, it is based on regular physical activity, sports, and a healthy lifestyle without bad habits.

The food pyramid began to be created by dieticians and scientists in the sixties. Then the doctors first discovered the balance, rationalism and useful components in the national cuisine of the Mediterranean. It was noted that the average life expectancy of the Mediterranean region was the highest on the entire continent, and at the same time, the rate of chronic and infectious diseases was well below the usual statistical expectations. Long-term studies and experiments led to the creation and publication of the Pyramid of Healthy Nutrition in 1993, which allowed the creation in the future of an ideal Mediterranean diet (the Pyramid diet).

So, let us study more in detail the basic principles of the Food Pyramid. At the base of the Pyramid, which contains the most important requirements for health and weight loss, is regular physical exercise and sport throughout the diet and then to consolidate the result. Thus, you need to do exercises every day, at least for 15-20 minutes.

Next is a list of products that should be included in the daily diet. They include vegetable products such as vegetables, fruits, as well as whole grains, potatoes, and legumes. It is recommended to add olive oil and other useful vegetable oil to these products. Also in the diet, including low-fat dairy products, such as cottage cheese, hard cheese, yogurt, kefir, etc. In addition, Mediterranean doctors say that every day you need to drink six glasses of ordinary unsalted mineral water. However, most importantly, you can afford two glasses of red wine.

In the middle of the pyramid are placed products that doctors allow to use 2-3 times a week. This list includes fish, mainly sea fish, seafood, poultry and chicken offal, as well as useful sweets, such as chocolate, cream ice cream, marshmallows, jam and jam, yogurt, marmalade, dried fruits, and fruit jellies.

At the top of the pyramid are placed meat products which, unfortunately, dieticians allowed to eat only 2-3 times a month.

In addition, you should know the following nuances of the Mediterranean diet:

1. You should reduce the consumption of salt and sugar, and replace them with natural seasonings, spices, lemon juice and apple cider vinegar;
2. You should use minimum processing of products, and it is desirable to use the ingredients raw and fresh, or processed steamed, cooked on the grill, stewed or boiled;
3. To ensure that your skin and hair are healthy, you should consume useful fats from olive oil, which can be added to salads, soups and side dishes. The number of other fats should not exceed 30% of your diet;
4. You should eat up to 7 eggs per week;
5. The entire volume of the daily diet should be divided into 3-5 small snacks;
6. You should not overeat or eat before going to bed;
7. If you break the rules and diet requirements, you will have to repeat the course of the diet;
8. The duration of the diet is not limited. Only your condition of your health and personal expectations from the process of losing weight can be limiting factors.

So, eat deliciously, take care of health, and lose weight forever!

Health Benefits of the Mediterranean Diet

The overweight problems frequently lead to serious health consequences such as cardiovascular diseases, mainly heart disease and stroke, and diabetes, muscular-skeletal injuries, such as osteoarthritis. These conditions cause premature death or disability. For these reasons, people who have overweight decide to change their lives, improve health, and increase the possibility of fulfilling themselves in a community. Therefore, this task is for everyone who wants to save a life and health.

However, everyone knows that weight loss will give you not only a beach-ready body. Weight loss will help improve your health, provide career development and increase your prosperity. In addition, this is only a few reasons for losing weight. Let us see what benefits will bring you Mediterranean diet and weight loss.

1. The Mediterranean diet help lose weight. People who consume a calorie-rich and healthy diet, such as olive oil, nuts, fatty fish, lose more weight than those who consider consumed calories but do not pay attention to the quality of the diet. To this conclusion came the scientists of the University of Barcelona. They called reducing fat in the diet the least effective way to lose weight.

2. The Mediterranean diet prolongs life. One of ten inhabitants of the Italian village of Acciaroli, located on the coast in the province of Salerno, lives up to 110 years. The National Geographic edition reports this fact. They argue that the secret of longevity, in this case, lies not only in a mild climate but also in an optimal food system. Numerous tests have shown that the menu of the inhabitants of Acciaroli contains a large amount of rosemary. In addition, another popular product is anchovies.

3. The Mediterranean diet improves brain function. Elderly people who followed the Mediterranean diet, improved activity and volume of the brain. It should be noted that the diet helps not only the elderly people!

4. The diet reduces the risk of developing cancer. According to researchers from the US Department of Veterans Affairs, the Mediterranean diet reduces the risk of developing breast cancer during life by 57%. It also has other obvious bonuses, for example, according to scientists, the risk of a heart attack and stroke, in this case, is reduced by 29% and the risk of type II diabetes by 30%.

5. The Mediterranean diet controls diabetes. The Mediterranean diet is able to stabilize the level of cholesterol and glucose in the blood, according to the "Daily Mail" which referring to recent studies in which about 3,000 people with diabetes already diagnosed took part. Moreover, this system of nutrition is equally useful to those who already live with diabetes and those who are at risk.

6. The diet protects a heart. People with cardiovascular diseases should use a diet that contains a large amount of olive oil, fresh vegetables, and nuts before the doctor prescribes them for superpotent substance treatment. So, in any case, believe Italian scientists who have established that the Mediterranean diet reduces the risk of death from heart and vascular disease by 37%.

7. The Mediterranean diet increases sexual activity. However, scientific data, which confirm this fact, is only in relation to men. As shown by experiments that were conducted at the University of California, a diet rich in useful fats and vitamins reduces the risk of developing erectile dysfunction. In addition, the Mediterranean diet increases the level of testosterone in men, contributing to sexual activity.

8. The Mediterranean diet prevents attention deficit and hyperactivity disorder. Attention deficit and hyperactivity disorder is a developmental disorder that begins in childhood. The study, published in the journal "Pediatrics", showed that children who have a lot of sugar and unhealthy fats in their diet are seven times more likely to suffer from a disorder than their peers. The scientists also managed to find out that children who rarely eat fish, olive oil, fruits, and vegetables, often show the general symptoms of the attention deficit and hyperactivity disorder.

9. The Mediterranean diet strengthens our bones. Women who follow the Mediterranean diet have a lower risk of hip fracture, in contrast to women who do not pay attention to their diet. Bavarian researchers who proved that the nutrients that are contained in Mediterranean products such as olive oil, yogurt, cheese, nuts, fresh vegetables and fruits, fish and poultry, grains and red wine could protect you from osteoporosis by preventing thinning of bone tissue made this conclusion.

10. The Mediterranean diet kills the symptoms of arthritis. According to a study by the University of Kent, the Mediterranean diet can reduce the markers of inflammation and improve the condition of the knee and hip joint in people who have arthritis. Data from one study that was conducted in Japan also showed that consumption of typical foods for the Mediterranean diet, in some cases, could suppress rheumatoid arthritis.

You should agree, for the sake of these pleasant moments should work hard for months or even years! You must try Mediterranean diet. Who knows perhaps and your way of life will radically change to the best for you!

Good luck and be healthy!

Reasons Why the Mediterranean Diet Truly Works for Weight Loss

The Mediterranean diet is not only the maintenance or loss of weight processes! It is an image of nutrition that is recognized by scientists as healthy and one of the best. Most of the foods that the diet included have anti-inflammatory and antioxidant properties.

According to WHO (World Health Organization) reports, the Spaniards, Italians, Greeks and French people populate the first seven countries with a healthy lifestyle.

Let us study the reasons for the effectiveness of the diet in more detail, and we will understand that the secret of losing weight lies in the chemical composition of healthy food, as well as in an active lifestyle.

Fats. The food contains a small amount of fat, about 30%. As a rule, it is only olive oil. The ratio between polyunsaturated (Vitamin F - omega-3 and omega-6) and monounsaturated fats is significant, 3: 1 or more. These substances our body receives from olive oil, which consists of 80% of oleic acid and is usually consumed with a huge amount of fresh vegetables and fruits.

Proteins. The amount of protein in the food is about 10%. Proteins in the diet come mainly from yogurts, cheeses, sea fish, eggs, and poultry. Fish, as well as olive oil, is an excellent source of omega-3 fatty acids, the benefits of which cannot be overemphasized.

Carbohydrates. The food contains a large number of carbohydrates, about 60%. In addition, the food is rich in fiber and carbohydrates with a low glycemic index. Carbohydrates are consumed mainly from vegetables and fruits. In addition, the food contains a large number of antioxidants, beta-carotene, and vitamins E and C.

Alcohol. It is believed that the use of red grape wines in moderate quantities is quite a common occupation for local residents. In addition, the positive effect of wine has antioxidants, which are found in grape seeds. Moreover, they contribute to reducing fat in cells and has a number of health benefits.

These beneficial properties of the diet, in conjunction with systematic exercise and quitting smoking, will save your heart and arteries healthy, and lower the risk of cardiovascular and other serious illnesses.

HOW the MEDITERRANEAN Diet HELP with WEIGHT LOSS

The Mediterranean diet is a balanced diet, so there are no medical contraindications for it. Despite the loyalty of this meal plan with regard to choice, combinations of foods and portions, however, the Mediterranean diet involves the rejection of a number of dishes. As a rule, it is fast food, semi-finished products, including ready-made factory sauces, refined products, and products containing hydrogenated fats.

However, every person who has ever tried to get rid of excess weight, it is clear that for weight loss you need to limit the number of calories! Only, in this case, our body will begin to spend its own fat reserves.

When making the menu of the Mediterranean diet, you should focus on the pyramid, which will help to make a diet in the right ratio! In addition, it is necessary to pay attention to the size of portions. For these purposes, you can use a volume measure of 1 cup, which equals 237 ml of liquid or 16 tablespoons.

In order to lose weight, nutrition experts recommend that you always evaluate the size of the dish. In any of the meals, one product is limited to the following volume:
1. Leafy fresh vegetables - 1 cup
2. Fresh, steamed or boiled vegetables - ½ cup
3. Pasta and any side dishes - ½ cup
4. Fresh, steam or boiled legumes - 1 cup
5. Yogurt or whole milk - 1 cup
6. Potatoes - 1 cup
7. Fruit - 1 piece
8. Egg - 1 piece
9. Nuts - 30 g
10. Lean meat or fish - 100 g

This, perhaps, is the only restriction offered by dietitians to those who want to lose weight on the Mediterranean diet. The specific composition of each breakfast, lunch, and dinner and the number of ingredients is determined by the weightiest, focusing on the proportions presented in the pyramid and the general recommendations of the nutrition plan. In addition, you should use a cookbook that is dedicated to losing weight with the help of the Mediterranean diet.

The Mediterranean diet also assumes five meals a day, of which three are full-fledged, namely breakfast, lunch, dinner, and two are just snacks. In addition, it is desirable to observe the same periods between meals.

In addition to healthy food, the Mediterranean is characterized by a variety of natural and physical activities, such as walking and cycling, team sport, and swimming! Therefore, physical activity is always an integral part of the answer to the question of how to lose weight with the help of the Mediterranean diet.

This is why I offer to you the Mediterranean diet cookbook, which is your chance to lose weight fast! Moreover, the Mediterranean diet is one of the famous ways to achieve effective results in losing weight and reduce the risk factors of various diseases. Therefore, if you are worried about your weight, health, and nutrition way, you should know that you are ready to change your usual life and give up the harmful food. Let us get rid of the overweight together!

The Importance of Exercise

Exercises and active lifestyle speed up metabolic process, oxygenate the cells, accelerate the lymph flow and circulation, improve digestion and help to eliminate toxins from the body through sweat. This is the ideal set of factors needed to reduce weight. In addition, exercises will help you lose weight, strengthen your muscles, increases immunity, improve the cardiovascular system, stimulate the production of a hormone of joy, and increase the level of endurance and strength of your body. There are the most effective sports that will help you quickly achieve the desired result. Let us discuss each of them.

Swimming. One of the most effective sports that helps to correct your figure. 1 hour of swimming will allow you to burn off up to 600 calories if you follow all the rules. You can swim with a trainer who will monitor the quality of the exercises and the process of weight reduction. Before the swim, you need to do a warm-up because it will help to avoid spasms and injuries.

Dancing. Perhaps, this is one of the most interesting sports with its bright varieties. One hour of training can burn off up to 500 calories and get many positive impressions. For girls, such weight loss will be especially pleasant, because they not only correct their figure but also realize their creativity.

Bicycle riding. This is the most effective method for those who want to correct the shape of the thighs and buttocks. You should ride a bicycle for only 30 minutes 3 times a week. In a month, you will notice how the excess weight disappears, and the muscles become elastic and elastic.

Run. There are different running techniques that help to lose weight. During running, you can burn off up to 750 calories in just 30 minutes. However, to achieve such results, you should do this kind of sport under the supervision of an instructor. Otherwise, you can get problems with muscles and joints.

Fitness. Rhythmic exercises are designed specifically to make your body ideal. Exercises suggest cardiac and anaerobic exercises, which combine to affect fat burning and the formation of strong muscles. As a rule, classes last for 1 hour, and you need to visit them 3 times a week.

Aerobics. This sport is designed specifically for weight loss. It combines complex exercises and dance elements, which makes training more diverse and interesting. In one lesson, you can lose up to 400 calories, which is an excellent indicator.

Even the most active workouts will not give the desired results if you do not comply with some rules of losing weight. Any sport should be combined with a balanced

Mediterranean diet. You should follow all the recommendations of coaches or instructors. In addition, you should remember that training should be regular because it is the only way to lose weight consistently.

7-DAY SAMPLE MEAL PLAN EXAMPLE

Monday	*Breakfast*	Wholemeal bun with olive oil and goat cheese + natural coffee with milk
	Lunch	Lentil soup, Greek salad with feta, 300 g of boiled buckwheat and a glass of kefir
	Snack	Fruit salad with yogurt and whole-grain toast
	Dinner	Omelet from 2 eggs, mushrooms, and vegetables + a glass of berries and citrus fresh juice
Tuesday	*Breakfast*	Milk soup with oatmeal and nuts + green tea with lemon
	Lunch	Salad, a portion of boiled brown rice, 2 whole-grain toast with olive oil + a glass of mineral water
	Snack	Curd casserole, 1 boiled egg.
	Dinner	Boiled rice with baked fish, vegetable salad + a glass of kefir
Wednesday	*Breakfast*	Brown rice with saffron and seafood + citrus fresh juice
	Lunch	Cold soup gazpacho, boiled buckwheat, and portions of stewed beef + yogurt

	Snack	Vegetable salad with nuts and chicken egg
	Dinner	Stewed beans, whole-grain toast with cheese and pomegranate + ginger drink
Thursday	Breakfast	Muesli with nuts and dried fruits + milk with cinnamon
	Lunch	Cream soup with broccoli, asparagus, and celery, boiled brown rice, fruit salad + yogurt
	Snack	Cottage cheese casserole with berries
	Dinner	Omelet with 2 eggs, mushrooms, and vegetables, a salad of red vegetables with nuts + green tea
Friday	Breakfast	Buckwheat porridge with milk, whole-grain toast with olive oil + natural grain coffee without sugar
	Lunch	Soup based on seafood and kelp, sprouted wheat and sour-fruit jelly
	Snack	Kefir with fruit added
	Dinner	Stewed beans, 2 whole-grain toast with goat cheese and grapefruit + herbal decoction.
Saturday	Breakfast	Milk chocolate with natural coffee and boiled oatmeal with yogurt
	Lunch	Chicken broth with vegetables, mashed potatoes, and steam chicken cutlets + fresh citrus juice
	Snack	2 marshmallows + yogurt
	Dinner	Greek salad with feta and nuts, 1 chicken egg and whole-grain toast with olive oil + green tea
Sunday	Breakfast	Boiled rice with dried fruits and nuts, whole-grain toast with goat cheese + herbal decoction
	Lunch	Vegetable soup, a portion of stewed cabbage with seafood + fruit juice

	Snack	Salad of berries, nuts, and yogurt
	Dinner	Stewed lentils with herbs and soy cottage cheese, whole-grain toast with olive oil + a glass of ginger drink

HEALTHY BREAKFAST

Strawberry breakfast

Ingredients (6 servings):

- 1 teaspoon of honey
- 2 pieces of toast
- 20 g butter
- 200 g strawberries
- 1 sprig of mint
- 3 tablespoons oat flakes

Cooking instruction:

As a first step, you should pour hot water 3 tablespoons oatmeal, cover and leave for 10 minutes. Then add the strawberries, honey, and mint. Smear the toast with butter and put the strawberries on top. Do not forget put mint leaves in the center. Then you should place sliced strawberries, honey, and fresh mint into hot green tea. Strawberry breakfast will give you a bright and cheerful mood for the whole day!
Bon Appetite!

Watermelon Gazpacho

Ingredients (12 servings):

- 1 kg of watermelon flesh
- 500 g of tomatoes
- 250 g of cucumbers
- 1 bundle of herbs
- basil or mint to taste
- pepper to taste
- salt to taste
- ground black pepper to taste
- 1 teaspoon of spicy sauce
- 2-3 soup spoons of juice of a lime
- 1-2 soup spoons of red wine vinegar
- olive oil

Cooking instruction:

As a first step, you should cut the vegetables and herbs. If you want to get a brighter color of gazpacho, previous peel the cucumbers. After that, place the chopped vegetables in a blender. The mass must be homogeneous. Remove the seeds from 1 kg of watermelon pulp and grind it in a blender. Combine the mixture of vegetables and herbs with crushed watermelon flesh. Next, you can add the watermelon to the vegetables gradually, by 1/3 chopped watermelon pulp at a time, mixing and tasting the soup. Add red wine vinegar, ground black pepper, juice of a lime, salt and hot sauce to taste and mix thoroughly. After that, place the soup in the refrigerator for 2-3 hours before serving. Well done!
   Bon Appetite!

Strawberry-citrus soup

Ingredients (3 servings):

- 500 g of strawberries
- 1 orange or lemon
- a sprig of fresh mint

Cooking instruction:

As a first step, you should squeeze the juice of orange or lemon. If you choose a lemon, you should grate the lemon zest on a grater. After that, you should rinse the strawberries and grind it in a blender until homogeneous mass forms. Now, you can refrigerate the strawberry mass in the fridge. You should add citrus juice to the soup before serving. Well done! You can decorate the soup with berries, bananas, lemon zest and a few leaves of fresh mint. Serve immediately.
Bon Appetite!

Omelet with vegetables and herbs

Ingredients (6 servings):

- 3 eggs
- 1 fresh red pepper
- 100 g of broccoli
- 2 medium-sized tomatoes
- 100 g of asparagus
- 150 g of any fresh herbs

Cooking instruction:

As a first step, you should oil and preheat a frying pan. After that, whisk the eggs in a deep bowl. Then chop one fresh red pepper, broccoli and tomatoes. Then add the chopped ingredients and asparagus in the deep bowl. You should mix the mass thoroughly. When the frying pan is heated, slowly pour the egg mixture. After that, you should evenly distribute the egg mass over the surface of the frying pan. Cook for 15 minutes. Do not forget to decorate the omelet with fresh herbs. Well done! Serve immediately!
    Bon Appetite!

Omelet with chicken breast

Ingredients (8 servings):

- 2 eggs
- 100 g of boiled chicken fillet
- 1 tomato
- 1 carrot
- 1 onion
- 2 teaspoons of sunflower oil
- salt to taste
- spices to taste

Cooking instruction:

As a first step, you should heat the oil in a pan and lightly fry the chopped onions, tomatoes and carrots. Then you should divide the meat into pieces. After that randomly lay the sliced meat and add salt and spices to taste. In addition, beat up the eggs and add a little salt. Stir well and pour into the frying pan. You should reduce the heat to a minimum, and cover the frying pan with a lid. The omelet should be cooked no more than 6-8 minutes. Well done!
    Bon Appetite!

Egg baked in avocado

Ingredients (3 servings):

- 8 eggs
- 4 avocados
- black pepper to taste

Cooking instruction:

As a first step, you should cut the avocado in half and remove the stones. Put the halves of the avocado on a baking sheet. After that, you should break the eggshell and pour the contents into each half of the avocado, so that the yolk is in the center. Then sprinkle with ground pepper and bake in the oven for 15-20 minutes. Well done!
Bon Appetite!

Italian frittata with vegetables

Ingredients (10 servings):

- 4 eggs
- 1 tomato
- 1 sweet pepper
- 1 onion
- 1 clove of garlic
- 1 bunch of parsley
- olive oil
- basil dried
- black pepper to taste
- salt to taste

Cooking instruction:

As a first step, you should chop the fresh parsley. Then beat the eggs. Stir eggs with chopped parsley. Leave the egg mixture for 5 minutes. At this time, you should fry the garlic in olive oil. Then add chopped onion, garlic, tomato and cook for another five minutes. Add the egg mixture and fry until the eggs are ready. After that, place the dish in the oven and bake until cooked at a temperature of 180 C. This will take about 15 minutes. Then add salt and pepper to taste. Do not forget to decorate the frittata with a dry basil. Well done!
Bon Appetite!

Pita bread rolls with bean salad and avocado

Ingredients (13 servings):

- pita bread
- 450 g of canned beans
- 2 avocados
- 2 tomatoes
- spinach, Peking cabbage, lettuce root to taste
- 4 sprigs of cilantro
- half of the chili pepper
- 1 clove of garlic
- 1 tablespoon of soy sauce
- 1 tablespoon of white wine vinegar
- 2 tablespoons the lime juice
- 1 teaspoon of sweet peppers
- salt, freshly ground black pepper to taste

Cooking instruction:

As a first step, you should wash beans with cold water, put them into a pan with olive oil, and fry over medium heat for 2 minutes. Add soy sauce and vinegar and continue frying and stirring until the liquid completely evaporates. After that, you should remove the beans from the fire and lightly mash with a fork. Avocado should be cut in half and removed the stone. Next, cut the flesh into small cubes and sprinkle with juice of a lime. Then you should chop the cilantro and garlic. Now, you can chop the pepper chili and tomatoes cut into small cubes. Then mix beans, avocados, chili pepper, cilantro, and garlic. Then add paprika, salt, and black pepper. Put the salad on the sheets of pita bread. Then put a layer of tomatoes, and lettuce leaves. Well done!
    Bon Appetite!

Greek style pumpkin

Ingredients (8 servings):

- 450 g pumpkin
- 0.5-1 teaspoon pepper mixture
- 0.5-1 teaspoon basil
- 0,5 tablespoon tomato paste
- 0.5-1 teaspoon of salt
- 2 tablespoons olive oil
- 2 cloves of garlic
- 2 tablespoons water

Cooking instruction:

As a first step, you should cut a pumpkin into large cubes. Do not take the number of pumpkins strictly according to the recipe. You can take more if you want. The main thing is that the pumpkin could be placed in one layer in a frying pan. Add olive oil to the frying pan and heat. Put the pieces of pumpkin and fry from all sides to a crispy crust. You can use sunflower oil if you want. Next, you need to fry the pumpkin with spices. You should add pepper, salt, dry basil, and tomato paste in a frying pan. Then chop the garlic, and add it to the pumpkin. Thoroughly mix all the ingredients and fry for 1 minute. Prepare a pumpkin baking dish. You can use glass or ceramic. After that, put the pumpkin fried with spices into a mold and add 2 tablespoons of water. Cover the baking dish with foil and place it in a preheated oven up to 180 °C. You should bake a pumpkin for 20-25 minutes. Well done!
    Bon Appetite!

Stuffed sweet potatoes

Ingredients (7 servings):

- 1 sweet potato
- 1 eggs
- ¼ of avocado
- 2 tablespoons of low-fat yogurt
- 2 tablespoons of salsa sauce
- fresh coriander to taste
- pepper to taste

Cooking instruction:

As a first step, you should heat the oven to 200 °C. Then place in the oven sweet potatoes and bake for 60 minutes. At the same time, you should whisk the eggs and the pepper to taste. The avocado should be cut into small pieces and coriander should be chopped. After that, cut baked sweet potatoes and carefully remove the core. Next, you should mash it with a fork and mix with the egg in a bowl. Heat the pan, add a little oil and fry the mixture of the pulp of sweet potatoes and eggs for several minutes on medium heat. Put fried mixture into the sweet potato, and then add cilantro, avocado, yogurt, and salsa. Well done!
    Bon Appetite!

Cauliflower with cream cheese and chicken

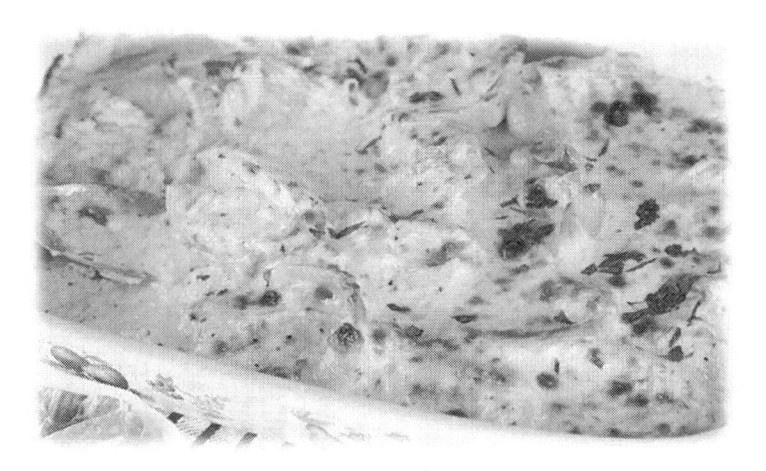

Ingredients (7 servings):

- 900 g of cauliflower
- 1 white onion
- 1 tablespoon of butter
- 120 g of cream cheese
- 120 ml of fatty cream
- 60 ml of chicken broth
- 1 tablespoon of grated cheese

Cooking instruction

As a first step, you should cut cauliflower into small pieces. Then put them in a saucepan with lightly salted water and cook on a medium heat for 20-30 minutes until they become soft and tender. Throw the vegetable in a colander and set it aside. Take a deep frying pan and melt butter on it. You should fry sliced white onions in the melted butter. Cook on a medium heat until the onion becomes soft. Then put cooked cauliflower on the bottom of the frying pan. After that, mix it with the onion. Next, chop the parts of cauliflower into smaller pieces. Reduce the heat and pour chicken broth and cream into the frying pan. Mix thoroughly. Then, add the cream cheese to the mixture. Stir the ingredients until the cheese has melted. If the contents of the frying pan are too thick, you can pour broth. Finally, sprinkle the contents of grated cheese and mix. After that, remove the frying pan from the heat. Now you should preheat the oven to about 160°C. Place the cauliflower along with the cream sauce into the baking dish, and sprinkle with grated cheese on top. You should bake for 15-20 minutes. Well done!
Bon Appetite!

FRUIT and BERRY DISHES

Fresh Berry soufflé

Ingredients (4 servings):

- 250 g of cottage cheese
- 50 g of berries to taste
- 15 g gelatin
- sugar substitute to taste

Cooking instruction:

As a first step, you should pour the gelatin 130 ml of boiling water and stir until dissolved. Then cool the gelatin. Mix gelatin with cottage cheese, add berries and sugar substitute. Mix thoroughly. For mixing, you can use a blender. Pour the mass into the forms and place in the fridge overnight. Do not forget to decorate the soufflé with fresh berries. Well done!
    Bon Appetite!

Cottage cheese - lime soufflé

Ingredients (6 servings):

- 250 g of cottage cheese
- 1 lime
- 3 eggs
- 3 tablespoons of milk
- 1 tablespoon of cornstarch
- 1 tablespoon of honey

Cooking instruction:

    As a first step, you should squeeze some lime juice and grate the zest on a grater. Then mash the cottage cheese, and add lime juice, zest, honey, starch, and milk. Mix all ingredients thoroughly. Then beat the eggs with a mixer until fluffy foam. Now, you should gently add the cheese, continuing to whisk the mass with a whisk. Preheat the oven to 190 °C. After that, you should put the cheese mass into the oiled baking dish for baking. You should bake for 30 minutes. Leave to cool in the oven. Well done! Serve immediately.
    Bon Appetite!

Bananas in batter

Ingredients (7 servings):

- 2 bananas
- 1 egg
- 3 tablespoons of flour
- 1 tablespoon of water
- 20 ml of lemon juice
- 0.5 teaspoons of baking powder
- vegetable oil

Cooking instruction:

As a first step, you should slice the bananas into small pieces and gently mix with lemon juice. For the batter, you should use the following products: egg, water, about 3-3.5 tablespoons of flour and baking powder. Thoroughly shake everything to make a mixture, similar to the dough for pancakes. Then slices of bananas, soaked in lemon juice, put into the flour, and then immerse the bowl filled with batter. Heat the vegetable oil in a frying pan and fry the bananas on both sides until a golden crust appears. Fried pieces put on a paper towel in order to remove excess oil. Well done! Serve the dish immediately. Do not forget to decorate with berries and fresh mint.
    Bon Appetite!

Grilled Fruits

Ingredients (7 servings):
- 3 apples
- 2 kiwis
- 300 g of melon
- 1-2 of tablespoons butter
- lemon juice to taste
- ginger ground to taste
- cinnamon powder to taste
- you also can add any berries, for example, 200 g of strawberry

Cooking instruction:

As a first step, you should melt butter over low heat. In addition, you can add ground ginger and cinnamon to taste. This basic mixture is well suited for apples, but for the cooking of kiwis and melons, you need to add a little lemon juice to the mixture. Lemon juice emphasizes the taste of fruit. Next, you should wash and dry apples. Then divide them into halves and remove the stone. Oil the fruit with melted butter. The oil will prevent the possibility of burning fruits, and delicately emphasize the natural taste of apples. Then you should cut the kiwis into slices. In a mixture of melted butter, add a little lemon juice to taste. After oil, the kiwi slices on all sides with the prepared mixture. For grilling, choose ripe but dense kiwis. In the process of grilling on the grill, even initially strong kiwis will become very soft, and too ripe kiwis may even turn into a homogeneous mass. Therefore, I recommend you to cut the kiwis no more than 2-4 slices. Slice the melon into slices. Then grease the slices on both sides with a mixture of melted butter and a little lemon juice. The fruit should steep for 5-7 minutes before proceeding to grill. Place the fruit on a well-heated grill surface. Bake the fruit on both sides until cooked. The cooking time can vary depending on what kind of fruit you use. Bake the bananas for 2-3 minutes, peaches 3-5 minutes, and melon for 7-10 minutes. Well done!
Bon Appetite!

Strawberry soufflé

Ingredients (3 servings):

- fresh strawberries to taste
- 10 g of edible gelatin
- lime juice

Cooking instruction:

As a first step, you should place the cranberries in a blender and simmer until a homogeneous mass form. Then add the gelatin and leave for a while. The mass should increase in size. Then preheat the strawberry mass by the double boiling until gelatin is dissolved, and then cool it to room temperature. Add the lime juice and whisk the mixer for 5-7 minutes. The mass should increase in size and become lighter by several tones and be enriched with oxygen. Then you should pour the strawberry mass into a mold and place it in the refrigerator until it freezes. Then take out the soufflé from the mold and cut into cubes. Well done! I think that you and your family will really like this dessert.
Bon Appetite!

Fresh pear soup

Ingredients (8 servings):

- 2 medium density pears
- 30 g butter creamy
- orange juice
- a pinch of a mixture of four peppers
- 0.5 pod of vanilla
- pinch of lime peel
- long straws of lime peel as soup decorations
- 1 sprig of fresh sage

Cooking instruction:

As a first step, you should wash, clean and remove seeds from the pear. Then cut the pear pulp into cubes of medium size and lightly fry in butter in a saucepan with a thick bottom. Add the orange juice, and bring to a boil. Then add a glass of hot drinking water and continue cooking on medium heat for 3-4 minutes. At the end of the cooking, add pepper, vanilla seeds and finely chopped lime. Then cook and stir for 30 seconds. After removing from heat. Well done! Before serving the soup, add sage leaves. Then decorate with lime. You can serve both hot and cold.

Bon Appetite!

Cheesecake with berries

Ingredients (4 servings):

- 500 g of cottage cheese
- 25 g of bran
- 150 g of berries to taste
- 3 egg whites
- 1 egg
- 1/2 teaspoon of cinnamon
- sugar substitute to taste

Cooking instruction:

As a first step, you should mix all the ingredients thoroughly in a large bowl. You can use a blender. After that, leave the mixture for 20 minutes at room temperature. You should place the mixture into the container of the slow cooker, and choose the mode of baking for 40 minutes. If you use the oven, you should bake for 40 minutes at 200 °C. Do not forget to decorate the cheesecake with fresh berries. Well done!
Bon Appetite!

Fruity smoothies

Ingredients (3 servings):

- 100 g of fresh plum
- 1 banana
- 1 orange

Cooking instruction:

As a first step, you should cut the plums in half and remove the stones. If the plums are large, you should cut the flesh into several pieces. After that remove the peel from the orange and divide it flesh into the slices. Next, you should peels and cuts banana into medium slices. Use a blender for mashing the sliced fruits. Mix all the ingredients in the blender thoroughly. Well done! Now you can pour the fresh smoothie into the glasses and serve immediately. If desired, several ice cubes can be added to the smoothie.
Bon Appetite!

Berry smoothies

Ingredients (5 servings):

- 200 g of fresh blackberry
- 2 apples
- 2 bananas
- 150 ml of water
- pinch of ground cinnamon

Cooking instruction:

    As a first step, you should cut the apples in half. Then you should cut the halves of the fruit into several pieces so that they quickly and finely grind. Bananas cut into rings. Then mix all the ingredients in a blender. Add the fresh black blackberry to the mass. Then add a little cold filtered water to the mass. After that, you should add a pinch of ground cinnamon to all ingredients. Once again, mix all ingredients in the blender. Pour the ready dessert into the glasses and decorate with berries of blackberry and a sprig of mint. Well done! Now you can enjoy the fruit explosion.
    Bon Appetite!

Smoothies with plum, banana, and orange

Ingredients (4 servings):

- 100 g of plum
- 1 banana
- 1 orange
- 1 tablespoon honey

Cooking instruction:

As a first step, you should cut the plums into halves and get the stone. If the plums are large, cut the flesh into several pieces. Remove the peel from the orange. Divide the flesh into slices. After that peels and cuts banana into slices. Cut the sliced fruit into a blender. Add the honey. If you are allergic or you just do not like honey, then replace it with another product, for example, agave syrup or Jerusalem artichoke, maple syrup or stevia. Mix all the ingredients in the blender. After pouring in the glasses and serve immediately. If desired, several ice cubes can be added to the smoothie.

Bon Appetite!

Mango, strawberry and Chia seeds

Ingredients (4 servings):

- 3 tablespoons of chia seeds
- 400 g of strawberries
- 3 bananas
- 1 mango

Cooking instruction:

As a first step, you should wash the strawberries. Then you should mash it in a mixer or blender. After that, add chia seeds to the strawberry mass. Thoroughly stir the mass and leave a minimum of 5 hours. The chia seeds must increase in size. Then cut fresh bananas and mangoes. You should mash all the ingredients in the mixer or blender. Now you can fill beautiful glasses with a homogeneous fruit mass. As a first step you should fill the glasses with banana mass, and then with strawberry. In addition, add the last banana layer. Decorate the masses with berries. Well done! You should eat dessert with mango, strawberries and chia seeds on an empty stomach or in the evening.
Bon Appetite!

Sherbet with melon and apple

Ingredients (6 servings):

- 4 glasses of chopped melon
- 1 cup of apple juice without sugar
- 1/4 cup of lime juice
- 1 glass of fresh or blueberries
- 1 glass of fresh or raspberries
- fresh mint leaves

Cooking instruction:

As a first step, you should place melon, apple juice and lime juice in a blender and mash them until the mass becomes homogeneous Transfer the finished product to a glass or metal container. Place the finished product in the freezer. Stir thoroughly every 30 minutes. After 3 - 4 hours, the sherbet should harden, but do not freeze. Sherbet should not contain lumps. After that, you can take the sherbet from the freezer. Using a large spoon, crush the fruit ice and place in a plastic container. Keep in the freezer for another 1 hour. Well done! Take the dessert from the freezer for 20 minutes, and then you can serve. Do not forget to decorate the dessert with berries and mint leaves.
    Bon Appetite!

FISH and SEAFOOD

Ceviche with langoustines

Ingredients (11 servings):

- 4 langoustines
- half a lemon
- 1 orange
- 1 chili pepper
- half a bow of red
- salt to taste
- greens to taste
- 0.5 teaspoon of olive oil
- 0.5 teaspoon of vinegar
- bay leaf to taste
- black pepper to taste

Cooking instruction

As a first step, you should squeeze the juice of lemon and orange. Then pour the juice into a deep container, in which you will pickle seafood. Then you should boil the water and add salt, pepper and bay leaf. Place the langoustines in a saucepan and cook for 1 to 2 minutes. Leave the seafood cool in the water for 15 minutes, so that the seafood soaked in the aroma of the broth. Then remove the langoustines and clean them from the shells. Be sure to remove the intestinal vein, which is in the tail of langoustine. Then move them to a bowl of juice and leave for 20 minutes. Now you should cut the orange pulp. After cutting half a red onion into small cubes. Do not forget to remove the seeds from the chili pepper! Gently cut and place it in a container with fresh herbs. Add a little vinegar and vegetable oil. Stir thoroughly. Now you can put the salad on a dish and decorate with lemon slices. Then add the pickled langoustines. Well done! Serve immediately!
    Bon Appetite!

Baked lobster with herbs

Ingredients (10 servings):

- 500 g of lobsters
- 1-2 cloves garlic
- 2 tablespoons of olive oil
- salt to taste
- black pepper to taste
- a few twigs of coriander
- a few twigs of parsley
- a few twigs of rosemary
- 1 tablespoon of lemon juice
- slices of lemon as desired

Cooking instruction

As a first step, you should finely chop the fresh herbs. After that put the chopped herbs into a deep bowl. Then you should crush the garlic and add it to the bowl. In addition, you should add olive oil and lemon juice. Add salt and pepper to taste. Stir all the ingredients thoroughly until a homogeneous mass appears. Put the lobsters into a dish. You should grease them with the sauce. Then leave the lobsters to marinate for a while, from time to time continue to grease by the sauce. Place the foil on the baking tray and lay out the lobsters. Now you should grease them with sauce again. Bake in preheated to 220°C oven for 10 minutes. After 5 minutes, you should turn over lobsters add the sauce on the other side. Well done! Serve immediately.
    Bon Appetite!

Trout baked with vegetables

Ingredients (9 servings):

- 1 kg of trout
- 100 g onion green
- 500 g cherry tomatoes
- 1 lemon
- 4 sprigs of thyme
- a couple of sprigs of parsley
- 2 tablespoons olive oil
- black pepper to taste
- spices for fish to taste

Cooking instruction

As a first step, you should remove the scales, the umbles, and gills. After that, you should wash the fish under running water, and dry with a paper towel. Place a piece of foil on the counter. Then oil the foil with olive oil. If you are afraid that the fish will still attach to the foil during baking, cut the onions with rings and place it on the foil, and then lay the fish on the onion layer. Sprinkle the fish with olive oil. Add pepper, and spices to the fish outside and inside the trout. Leave the fish for a few minutes to marinate. Stuff the fish with a sprig of parsley, a couple of twigs of thyme, green onions, cherry tomatoes and lemon. Bake in preheated oven to 180 degrees for 20 minutes. Well done! Trout baked in the oven, serve immediately after baking.
    Bon Appetite!

Provence Dorade with Tapenade

Ingredients (4 servings):

- 2-3 sprigs of basil
- 100 g of classical tapenade
- 2 tomatoes
- 2 medium sized Dorade fish

Cooking instruction

As a first step, you should cut the tomatoes and then blanch them in boiling water for 30 seconds. After placing the tomatoes in cold water. Then remove the seeds, and chop the flesh into long pieces. Add salt and pepper. The fish should be headed and gutted. In addition, you should thoroughly wash it inside and out. Then dry the fish with a paper towel. After that, cover the fish with olive oil on one side and cover with a layer of tapenade on the other. Put the fish on a baking tray. The oily side of the fish should lie on a baking sheet. Then you should put tomato slices on top of the fish. Bake in the oven preheated to 200 ° C for 15-20 minutes. Before serving, do not forget to decorate with fresh basil. Well done!
    Bon Appetite!

Delicious shrimp

Ingredients (8 servings):

- 1 kg of peeled shrimp
- 3 tablespoons of honey
- 6 tablespoons of olive oil
- 3 cloves of pressed garlic
- 50 ml of lime juice
- lime peel
- black pepper to taste
- fresh herbs to taste

Cooking instruction:

As a first step, you should place honey, olive oil, lime juice, pressed garlic, and lime peel in a bowl to make a marinade for shrimp. Then mix them well. After that, place peeled shrimp in the bowl with a marinade. Then, put the bowl in the refrigerator for 30 minutes. In 30 minutes, remove the bowl from refrigerator and leave it at room temperature for 15 minutes. After that, you should place the shrimp in a preheated frying pan. You should fry the shrimp until they become golden. Do not forget to turn them to the other side. Well done! In addition, use fresh herbs to your taste.
      Bon Appetite!

Baked seafood with vegetables and lemon

Ingredients (12 servings):

- 50 g of butter
- 2 carrots
- 1/2 of lemon (peel and juice)
- 3-4 sprigs of chopped dill
- black pepper to taste
- 30 g of soy sauce
- laurel leaf to taste
- 2 tomatoes
- 2 onions
- 30 g of lemon juice
- 500 g of seafood
- 5 tablespoons of vegetable oil

Cooking instruction

As a first step, you should defrost the seafood by placing them on the top shelf of the refrigerator. Grate the carrot and cut the onion into cubes. Then a little salt and fry in vegetable oil for 10-12 minutes until the appearance of golden color. After that, you should cut the tomatoes and lemon into circles. Put tomatoes on the foil, then carrots and onions. On top of the layer of vegetables, put seafood, sprigs of dill and 2-3 circles of lemon. Add the bay leaves and black pepper to taste. Do not forget to melt the butter and mix it with lemon juice and soy sauce. Add the mixture to vegetables and seafood. Tightly wrap the envelope from the foil and place it in the oven. Bake in the oven for 10-12 minutes. Well done!

       Bon Appetite!

Mussels with vegetables

Ingredients (7 servings):
- 700 g of mussels
- 100 g of celery
- 100 g of leeks
- 100 g of carrots
- 70 g of onions
- 350 ml of beer
- 10 g of parsley

Cooking instruction

As a first step, you should slice the celery into small pieces, and cut the carrots into slices. After that, put the vegetables in a deep pan or a saucepan. After that, you should cut onion and leek into rings. Place the chopped onion and leek into the saucepan. Add the beer to the vegetables and put the pan on the fire. You should simmer the vegetables in the beer for 10-12 minutes. The vegetables should be soft. If it is necessary add salt to taste. While the vegetables are cooking, you should wash the mussels. Remove sand and shards of shells. All the opened mussels need to be thrown out. After that, put mussels in a pot with vegetable broth and close the saucepan by a lid. Stew the mussels for 5-7 minutes. Closed mussels should open. Take the saucepan by the handles and shake it a little so that all the mussels are in the broth. Put mussels in plates and pour them with sauce. Well done!

Bon Appetite!

PASTA & SOUPS

Baked pasta with minced meat

Ingredients (13 servings):

- 1 kg of ground beef,
- 800 g of tomatoes,
- 500 g of penne pasta,
- 400 g of marinara sauce,
- 400 g ricotta,
- 400 g of mozzarella cheese,
- 1 large onion,
- 1 egg,
- 3 cloves garlic,
- 2 tablespoons of olive oil,
- 2 teaspoons of a mixture of Italian herbs,
- ½ teaspoon of coarse-grained red pepper,
- salt and black pepper to taste.

Cooking instruction:

As a first step, you should finely chop onion and garlic. Then fry them in olive oil. Add ground beef and constantly stirring until the excess moisture evaporates. When stuffing a little fry, add tomatoes and marinara sauce. Then add Italian mixture, red, black pepper, and salt. Stew the dish for half an hour. In 30 minutes, move a third of the sauce from the frying pan into a separate bowl. Also, combine the ricotta, grated mozzarella and eggs in a separate bowl. Add salt, pepper, and whisk until smooth. After that, cook the pasta. After rinsing the pasta under cold running water. Mix with ground meat and cheese. Next, you should put everything in a glass container. After that, add the tomato-meat sauce, and sprinkle with grated cheese. You should bake the pasta at 190 °C. The cooking time takes about 2-2.5 hours.
    Bon Appetite!

Lasagne alla Bolognese

Ingredients (14 servings):

- pasta sheets of lasagna
- 500 g of minced beef
- 1 carrot
- 1 onion
- 3 cloves of garlic
- 2 tomatoes
- salt to taste
- basil to taste
- a mixture of peppers to taste
- herbes de Provence to taste
- 4 tablespoons of butter
- 4 tablespoons of flour
- 500 ml of milk
- 300 g of cheese

Cooking instruction:

As a first step, you should fry in olive oil one finely chopped onion and one grated carrot. Add 500 g of minced meat and 2-3 cloves of garlic to the frying pan. Then add sliced tomatoes with peeled skin. All ingredients should be stewed for 10-15 minutes. At the same time, you should add salt, a mixture of peppers, herbes de Provence, and basil. Now you should make a bechamel sauce. You should melt four tablespoons of butter in a saucepan. Then add four tablespoons of flour. You should mix thoroughly to ensure that there are no lumps. Then gradually add 500 ml of milk. Do not forget to mix the mass. Add salt to taste. The process of thickening the sauce takes 10 minutes. Well done! Then oil the bottom of the baking dish and lay dry pasta sheets of lasagna on the bottom. Then put a layer of minced meat. Next, pour the sauce over the béchamel and sprinkle with grated cheese. You should alternate the layers until the baking dish is filled completely. The last layer should include pasta sheets of lasagna, béchamel sauce, and grated cheese. Bake in the oven for 30 minutes at 200 °C. Well done! Serve immediately!
    Bon Appetite!

Manicotti with light pasta sauce

Ingredients (10 servings):

- 1 ½ cups of tasty light pasta sauce
- 12 dry manicotti noodle products
- 1¾ cup of ricotta cheese
- 1 package of spinach
- ¼ cup of cut thin Parmesan cheese
- an egg white
- a teaspoon of powdered garlic
- a teaspoon of dried basil
- a teaspoon of dried oregano
- ¼ cup of cut thin mozzarella cheese (no fat)

Cooking instruction:

As a first step, you should preheat the oven to approximately 350 C°. Oil the baking pan with a special culinary spray. Then you should fill the dish with ½ cup of light pasta sauce. You should cover only the bottom of the dish. Then bring to a boil a saucepan filled with salted water. Manicotti should be prepared according to the instructions for cooking indicated on the package. In a bowl, combine ricotta cheese, spinach, Parmesan cheese, egg white, powdered garlic, dried basil and dried oregano according to the list of ingredients. Use a mixture of cheeses to fill the manicotti noodle products. Then move them to the prepared baking dish. After that, you should fill the baking dish with a bowl of pasta sauce. It is necessary to cover the baking dish with foil. The baking process takes approximately 20 minutes. Use the cut thin mozzarella cheese for uncovering of manicotti noodle products and bake for 5 minutes. Well done!
    Bon Appetite!

Spaghetti Carbonara

Ingredients (9 servings):

- 2 teaspoon of salt
- 1 ¼ teaspoon of black pepper
- 2 pounds of spaghetti
- slices of bacon
- garlic to taste
- 2 eggs yolks
- 1 whole egg
- a cup of grated Parmesan cheese
- 100 ml of cream

Cooking instruction:

As a first step, you should cut bacon into thin strips. Then finely chop the peel garlic. Also, cut clean and dry herbs. Bacon in a deep frying pan or saucepan. Use medium heat. Bacon you should cook approximately 3 minutes. Then add garlic and fry for 2 minutes. Add parsley and black pepper. Mix thoroughly and remove the saucepan from the heat. Combine the following ingredients in the bowl: egg yolks, cream, grated Parmesan, salt, and pepper. It is necessary to mix well the creamy sauce. Cook the spaghetti according to the cooking instruction, which indicated on the pack. Ready to use spaghetti combine with bacon. Mix the mass. Then add the creamy sauce to the spaghetti. It is necessary to mix well the creamy sauce with the spaghetti. Well done! Remove the saucepan with the pasta from the heat and immediately serve it to the table. Sprinkle the carbonate spaghetti with parsley and grated Parmesan cheese.
    Bon Appetite!

Pasta with low-fat cheese

Ingredients (7 servings):

- 150 g of pasta
- 50 g of grated cheese
- ½ cup of yogurt without flavorings
- 50 of fresh spinach or other herbs to your taste
- pepper to taste
- ¼ tablespoon of onion powder
- ¼ tablespoon of garlic powder

Cooking instruction:

As a first step, you should cook the pasta. When the pasta is cooked, you should drain water from a pot into a cup. After that, place the leaves of fresh spinach or any herbs to your taste to the cooked pasta. Now, you should add approximate 1/4 cup of pasta water to the pot. Next, add grated cheese. Mix up the mass with the cheese until it melts. Then add yogurt without flavorings, onion powder, garlic powder, and pepper to taste. Mix the mass thoroughly. The mass should be homogeneous. Well done! Serve immediately.
   Bon Appetite!

Pasta with salmon and shrimp

Ingredients (10 servings):

- 300 g of peeled shrimp
- 200 g of salmon
- 3 cloves of garlic
- 2 tablespoons olive oil
- 200 g of tomatoes
- 40 g of grated cheese
- 5 sprigs of parsley
- 3 sprigs of basil
- pepper to taste
- 250 g of spaghetti

Cooking instruction:

As a first step, you should cook spaghetti in salted water for 8-12 minutes. Then drain the water. After that, finely chop the garlic. Heat up the pan. Add the oil and fry the garlic. Place the chopped tomatoes in the pan and simmer for 5 minutes. Slice the salmon fillet, if necessary remove bones. Add to tomato sauce salmon and shrimp. After adding the pepper to taste. Cover the pan with a lid and simmer for 10-12 minutes. Add grated cheese, stir and cook for another two-three minutes. After that, you need finely chopped herbs. Add pasta and herbs to the sauce. Mix thoroughly. Well done!
    Bon Appetite!

Gazpacho with tomato juice and Tabasco sauce

Ingredients (10 servings):

- 4 tomatoes
- 2 red peppers
- 1 fresh cucumber
- 8 cloves of garlic
- 5 glasses of tomato juice
- ¼ cup of red vinegar
- ¼ cup of olive oil
- ½ teaspoons of Tabasco sauce
- black pepper to taste
- salt to taste

Cooking instruction:

As a first step, you should preheat a frying pan. After that, fry garlic with husks without sunflower oil on a medium heat. In 10 - 15 minutes, the garlic should become soft and black in several places. Remove the frying pan from the heat, and allow the garlic to cool. Then chop the red sweet pepper into medium sized pieces, as well as a large cucumber, and ripe tomatoes without the skin. The cooled garlic to peel off the husk. Put the garlic and tomatoes in a blender, and grind until a homogeneous mass is formed. Then put the mass in a bowl. Then grind the peppers and cucumber. Stir all ingredients thoroughly. You should add tomato juice, as well as spices, red vinegar and Tabasco sauce. Stir all ingredients thoroughly again. Well done! You should serve the dish cold.
    Bon Appetite!

Cream soup with pumpkin and French bean

Ingredients (8 servings):

- 100 g of French bean
- 4 potatoes
- 3 carrots
- 1 onion
- 50 g of pumpkin
- fresh herbs
- pepper to taste
- olive oil

Cooking instruction:

The cup of French bean must be placed in a glass of water for the night. One cup of French bean needs four cups of water. After that, you should cook the French bean about half an hour. Cut the pumpkin into cubes and add to the French bean. Then add the chopped potatoes, onions and carrots. You should boil the vegetables until they become soft. After that, you should put the contents of the pan into a blender and grind well all the ingredients. Now, you can add the olive oil and pepper to taste. Next, you should cook the soup for another 10 minutes. Well done!
    Bon Appetite!

Vegetable cream soup

Ingredients (6 servings):

- 500 g of cauliflower
- 500 g of broccoli
- 6 glasses of vegetable broth
- 1/2 of onion
- 1 tablespoon of olive oil
- 1/2 teaspoon of salt

Cooking instruction:

As a first step, you should divide cauliflower and broccoli into pieces. Then you should finely chop the onion. Heat the olive oil in a frying pan and fry chopped onion for 7-8 minutes. Ready to use vegetable broth pour into a large saucepan and bring to a boil. Then, you can add at the same time all vegetables, and salt to taste. Reduce heat and cook for half an hour. Then remove the soup from the heat, and cool it a little. After that, pour the contents of the saucepan into a blender and grind all the ingredients until a homogeneous mass is obtained. Well done! You can decorate the soup with fresh herbs or boiled broccoli at will.
    Bon Appetite!

Green cream soup

Ingredients (6 servings):

- 400 g of broccoli
- 1 tablespoon of grated cheese
- 200 ml of low-fat cream
- 1 teaspoon of butter
- 1 white onions
- 1l of chicken broth

Cooking instruction:

As a first step, you should melt the butter in the frying pan. Then slice the onion and fry it. Slices of onion should become golden and soft. After that, add the chicken broth to the frying pan. You should cook on a medium heat until the broth boils. Now, you can add chopped broccoli. Then the content should boil again. After that, reduce the heat. Cook the soup until the broccoli becomes soft. After that, you can remove the frying pan from the heat. All the ingredients should be placed in the blender for grinding. Well done! Next, you should add to the ground ingredients low-fat cream and grated cheese. Mix the mass with help of blender again. The soup should be served immediately.
    Bon Appetite!

HEALTHY SALADS

Salad with avocado, pineapple, and onions

Ingredients (4 servings):

- 1 avocado
- 1 onion
- 6 slices of pineapple
- 1 lemon

Cooking instruction:

As a first step, you should chop the onion rings. Then the avocado should be cut into small cubes. Now, you can add the lemon juice and mix thoroughly. After that, chop the pineapple into small pieces. Then, you should fry it in sunflower oil until they become golden. Next, you should cool the fried pineapple down. Then place the avocado, pineapple, onion in a bowl and add a little olive oil and the lemon juice. Mix thoroughly. Add the pepper to taste. Well done! Serve immediately.
    Bon Appetite!

Salad with shrimp

Ingredients (6 servings):

- 2 eggs
- 200 g of shrimps peeled
- olive oil
- black ground pepper to taste
- paprika to taste
- fresh herbs to taste

Cooking instruction:

As a first step, you should boil the eggs in salted water. Then peel off the shell and finely chop the boiled eggs. After that, you should mix the chopped eggs with boiled shrimp in a bowl. Now you can add a few tablespoons of olive oil to the salad. Mix all the ingredients thoroughly. Next, you should add the ground paprika and black pepper. Well done! Do not forget to decorate the salad with twigs of fresh herbs. Serve immediately.
    Bon Appetite!

Salad with watermelon, cheese, and fresh basil

Ingredients (6 servings):

- 50 g feta
- fresh basil
- 2 tablespoons of olive oil
- 1 teaspoon of wine vinegar
- 1/2 of onion
- 100 g of watermelon flesh

Cooking instruction:

As a first step, you should chop the flesh of the watermelon into cubes. Then remove all the seeds from the watermelon flesh. In addition, you should cut feta cheese into cubes and place them in a bowl with the watermelon cubes. After that, you should add the chopped onion and fresh basil. Now, you can add olive oil, crushed red pepper, vinegar and mix all the ingredients thoroughly. Well done! Serve immediately.
    Bon Appetite!

Salad with fresh vegetables

Ingredients (10 servings):

- fresh broccoli
- 2 fresh tomatoes
- 1 fresh cucumbers
- 1 fresh sweet pepper
- 3 tablespoons of olive oil
- lemon juice
- pepper to taste
- 1 cloves of garlic
- 1-2 radishes
- fresh herbs to taste

Cooking instruction

As a first step, you should chop tomatoes, cucumber, sweet pepper and radishes into pieces. In addition, break the fresh broccoli into small pieces. After that, put all the chopped vegetables in a large bowl. Now, you should add the olive oil and lemon juice to the vegetables. Mix thoroughly. Then add the pepper to taste and mix well the chopped vegetables again. Next, you should crush the garlic and add to all the ingredients in the bowl. In addition, you can add the chopped herbs to taste. Thoroughly stir. Well done! Serve immediately!
   Bon Appetite!

Salad with cod liver and quail eggs

Ingredients (9 servings):

- 6 quail eggs
- 1 cucumber
- 100 g of olives
- 1 teaspoon of sesame seeds
- fresh herbs
- 3 tablespoons of olive oil
- 1 tablespoon of lemon juice
- ground black pepper to taste
- 250 g of cod liver

Cooking instruction

As a first step, you need to make the sauce. For that, you should mix olive oil and lemon juice in a large bowl. Then add black pepper and mix thoroughly. After that, you should boil the quail eggs for 10 minutes. Then cut them in half. Now, you can split the cod liver with a fork into large pieces. Next, cut the cucumber into thin rings or strips. In addition, finely chop the fresh herbs. After that, you should mix cucumber strips with the fresh herbs. Now, you can put pieces of cod liver, olives, and quail eggs. Add sauce and fried sesame seeds. Well done! Serve immediately.
    Bon Appetite!

Salad with shrimps and olives

Ingredients (9 servings):

- 300 g of shrimps
- 150 g of olives
- 1 lemon
- 1 onion
- 4 tablespoons of olive oil
- fresh herbs to taste
- 100 g of lettuce
- 5 cherry tomatoes
- pepper to taste

Cooking instruction

As a first step, you should boil the water in a saucepan. Then place the fresh shrimps in the boiling water. After that, add a little lemon juice. Stir well. In 1 minute after boiling, remove the saucepan from the heat. Now, you can place boiled shrimps in a bowl. Then add the chopped black olives, cherry tomatoes, and leaves of lettuce. After that, you should add olive oil and lemon juice. Stir well and add pepper to taste. In addition, you can decorate the shrimps with lemon slices and fresh herbs to taste. Well done!
    Bon Appetite!

Salad with lentils and avocado

Ingredients (10 servings):

- 2 tablespoons of olive oil
- 2 tablespoons of lemon juice
- 1 g of mustard
- 1/2 teaspoons of honey
- 1 onion
- 1 bell pepper
- 10 cherry tomatoes
- 1 avocado
- fresh herbs to taste
- 3/4 cup of lentils

Cooking instruction

As a first step, you should boil the lentils according to the instructions on the package. Then, finely chop the onion and cut the tomatoes into quarters. After that, you should add the cooled lentils and chopped into cubes pepper. In addition, add the cubed avocado. Now, you can place all ingredients in a bowl. After that, you should add the sauce, fresh herbs, and pepper to taste. Stir thoroughly. Well done! Serve immediately.
    Bon Appetite!

Salad with Brussels sprouts, apples and nuts

Ingredients (11 servings):

- Brussels sprouts
- 1 apple
- 1/2 lemon
- fresh mint
- fresh basil
- 2 tablespoons of olive oil
- 2 tablespoons of walnut oil
- 1 tablespoon of apple cider vinegar
- 1 teaspoon of mustard
- Hazelnuts to taste
- black pepper to taste

Cooking instruction

As a first step, you should heat the olive oil in a frying pan. Then add the Brussels sprouts and fry until they become golden brown. After that, cut the apple into thin slices. Add lemon juice to the chopped apple. Then place the Brussels sprouts in a deep bowl and add the mustard, apple cider vinegar, walnut oil, lemon juice, and pepper to taste. Thoroughly mix all the ingredients. Now, you should dry hazelnuts in a frying pan and then grind them. Now you can finely chop the mint and basil. After that, you should add the apple, mint, and basil to the Brussels sprouts and mix thoroughly. Now you can add the hazelnuts. Well done! Serve immediately.
    Bon Appetite!

Salad with shrimps and quail eggs

Ingredients (11 servings):

- 300 g of shrimps
- 150 g of black olives
- 1 lemon
- 1 onion
- 3 soup spoons of vinegar
- 5 quail eggs
- 50 g of herbs
- 100 g of lettuce
- 3 soup spoons of olive oil
- 5 cherry tomatoes
- pepper to taste

Cooking instruction

    As a first step, you should marinate the chopped onion in vinegar for 20-30 minutes. Then boil the water in a saucepan and throw in boiling water fresh shrimps. Net pour a little lemon juice. In 1 minute after boiling, remove the saucepan from the heat. Then boil the quail eggs. You should cook quail eggs for 3 minutes after boiling. After that, cool the eggs under cold water and then clean them from the shell. Now you can place the ingredients in a bowl and add the chopped black olives, cherry tomatoes, and leaves of fresh lettuce. After that, add olive oil and lemon juice. In addition, you can decorate the shrimps with lemon slices, herbs, quail eggs and pepper to taste. Well done! Serve immediately!
    Bon Appetite!

Salad with lentils and trout

Ingredients (9 servings):

- 1 teaspoon of mustard
- 1/2 teaspoon of lemon juice
- fresh dill
- 200 g of lightly salted trout
- 125 g of yogurt without flavorings
- 1 avocado
- 3 tomatoes
- green onions
- 50 g of lentils

Cooking instruction

As a first step, you should pour the lentils with water and simmer over low heat for 20 minutes after boiling. Then drain the water, put the lentils on a flat plate, and cool down. Cut avocado in half and remove the stone. After that, you should chop the flesh of the avocado into cubes. Add lemon juice. Now, you can chop the tomatoes into cubes. Next, remove the bones of the trout. Grind the sliced trout and all ingredients for the sauce in a blender. After that, you should chop green onions finely. Then put the chopped tomatoes, avocado, and lentils in a bowl. Add the sauce. Stir well. Do not forget to decorate the salad with green onions. Well done! Serve immediately.
    Bon Appetite!

Conclusion

Healthy eating is one of the fundamental moments of our healthy lifestyle and, consequently, the preservation and strengthening of our health. This significant and constantly acting factor ensures adequate growth and development of our body. Rational healthy nutrition provides us with adequate physical and neuropsychological development, increases resistance to infectious diseases and resistance to unfavorable environmental conditions. Most of our population is neglectful about their health. Lack of time, incompetence in the issues of food culture, the pace of modern life led us to illegibility in the choice of food.

Many people believe that eating healthy is a difficult habit. However, a healthy diet has benefits, most of which you can see immediately after switching to healthy food. Healthy diet and diet give us great benefits for physical and mental health. A healthy diet does not mean that we should starve! We just need to balance the intake of proteins, fats, and carbohydrates.

Increased energy levels are a direct advantage of switching to a healthy diet. In addition, eliminating excess fats and carbohydrates helps prevent changes in blood glucose levels.

A healthy diet increases blood flow to the brain, protecting brain cells from damage, and helps prevent Alzheimer's disease. For brain health, you should avoid fried foods, and consume more fruits and vegetables such as cabbage, spinach, broccoli, prunes, raisins, blueberries, raspberries, plums, and cherries. Almonds, walnuts, pecans and other nuts are a source of vitamin E, which along with other vitamins also helps fight Alzheimer's disease.

Take care and be healthy!

Author's Afterthoughts

Thanks ever so much to each of my cherished readers for investing the time read this book!

I know you could have picked from many other books but you chose this one. So big thanks for downloading this book and reading all way to the end.

If you enjoyed this book or received value from it, I'd like to ask you for a favor. Please take a few minutes to post an honest and heartfelt review on Amazon.com Your support does make a difference and to benefit other people.

Made in the USA
Middletown, DE
21 May 2018